MINISTRY OF MUNITIONS

Technical Department—Aircraft Production.

FOKKER.

I.C. 640.

Kingsway, W.C.2.

REPORT ON

FOKKER

SINGLE-SEATER BIPLANE. D.VII.

September, 1918.

The Naval & Military Press Ltd

Published by
The Naval & Military Press Ltd
5 Riverside, Brambleside, Bellbrook
Industrial Estate, Uckfield, East Sussex,
TN22 1QQ England

Tel: +44 (0) 1825 749494
Fax: +44 (0) 1825 765701

www.naval-military-press.com
www.military-genealogy.com

*In reprinting in facsimile from the original, any imperfections are inevitably reproduced
and the quality may fall short of modern type and cartographic standards.*

MINISTRY OF MUNITIONS

Technical Department—Aircraft Production.

FOKKER.

I.C. 640.

KINGSWAY, W.C.2.

REPORT ON
FOKKER
SINGLE-SEATER BIPLANE. D.VII.

SEPTEMBER, 1918.

T.5. 974/5675. 17/9/1918.

Report on the Fokker Single-Seater Biplane.

The British No. of the machine is G/2B/14, and the German No. is Type D7 F.N. 1,450; maker's No. 2,455.

It was brought down north of Hazebrouck on June 6th, 1918, by a British S.E.5a, and is a single-seater fighter.

The principal dimensions are as follows:—

Span	29 ft.	3½ ins.
Chord (upper wing)	5 ,,	2¼ ,,
Chord (lower wing)	3 ,,	11¼ ,,
Overall length	22 ,,	11½ ,,
Gap	4 ,,	2 ,,
Area of Upper Wings (with ailerons)	140.7 sq. ft.	
,, ,, Lower Wings	78.3 ,, ,,	
,, ,, Aileron (one only)	5.7 ,, ,,	
,, ,, Balance of Aileron	.5 ,, ,,	
,, ,, Horizontal Tail Plane	21.1 ,, ,,	
,, ,, Elevators	15.2 ,, ,,	
,, ,, Balance of Elevator	1.1 ,, ,,	
,, ,, Fin	2.8 ,, ,,	
,, ,, Rudder	5.9 ,, ,,	
,, ,, Horizontal Area of Body	35.6 ,, ,,	
,, ,, Vertical Area of Body	58.6 ,, ,,	
,, ,, Plane between wheels	12.4 ,, ,,	

This aeroplane presents features of very great interest, whether viewed from the standpoint of aerodynamic design or of actual construction. The machine which has been the subject of investigation was unfortunately rather extensively damaged, thus making absolute accuracy of description difficult, and trials of performance impossible.

A similar machine, however, has been tested for performance by the French authorities, who have issued the following report:—

Altitude.	Time of climb.	Speed at this height.
1000 metres (3281 feet)	4 mins. 15 secs.	116.6 m.p.h.
2000 ,, (6562 ,,)	8 ,, 18 ,,	114.1 ,,
3000 ,, (9843 ,,)	13 ,, 49 ,,	109.7 ,,
4000 ,, (13124 ,,)	22 ,, 48 ,,	103.5 ,,
5000 ,, (16405 ,,)	38 ,, 5 ,,	94.9 ,,

There are many points in which there is distinct divergence from accepted German, and tendency towards British, practice. The undercarriage, position of radiator, and aileron control levers, or kingposts, are examples.

This fact is some indication that the designer of this machine has approached the various problems and compromises which confront one who sets out to create such a machine, with a quite open mind, and, if this be allowed, there is a very strong case for a thorough investigation of those features which are in contradiction to contemporary British practice. These points include the wing design, which is without any external bracing but of especially deep section; the steel-tubular fuselage, and the peculiar bracing of this member.

There is nothing to prevent the adoption of the first and last features; but it should be pointed out with regard to the steel work that experienced welders have expressed the opinion that this art has been developed by the enemy to a high degree of efficiency. Indeed, the welding is sufficiently good to give rise to the belief that new methods, involving radical changes, have been adopted.

*The following data regarding weights is taken from a French source:—

Weight of fuselage, complete with engine, etc.	1322.2 lbs.
,, ,, upper wing with ailerons	167.2 ,,
,, ,, lower wing	99.0 ,,
,, ,, fin and rudder	6.6 ,,
,, ,, fixed tail plane	17.6 ,,
,, ,, elevators	9.9 ,,
	1622.5 lbs.

A different French report gives the following figures, which are taken from inscriptions found on one of the Spandau guns on a captured Fokker of the same type:—

Weight, empty	1540 lbs.
Permissible load (useful load and fuel)	396 lbs.

WINGS.

As in the Fokker triplane, the extreme depth of wing section and the absence of external bracing are distinctive features. Both upper and lower wings are without dihedral, and are in one piece. The way in which the lower wings are fitted into their place is described in detail under the heading "Fuselage." Both upper and lower chords are set parallel to the crankshaft, i.e., at no angle of incidence, and the inscription "Angle of incidence, 0°" is painted on the upper plane.

---

*The schedule of principal weights given on page 12, is the result of weighing the actual components mentioned, which were taken from the aeroplane allotted G/2B/14.

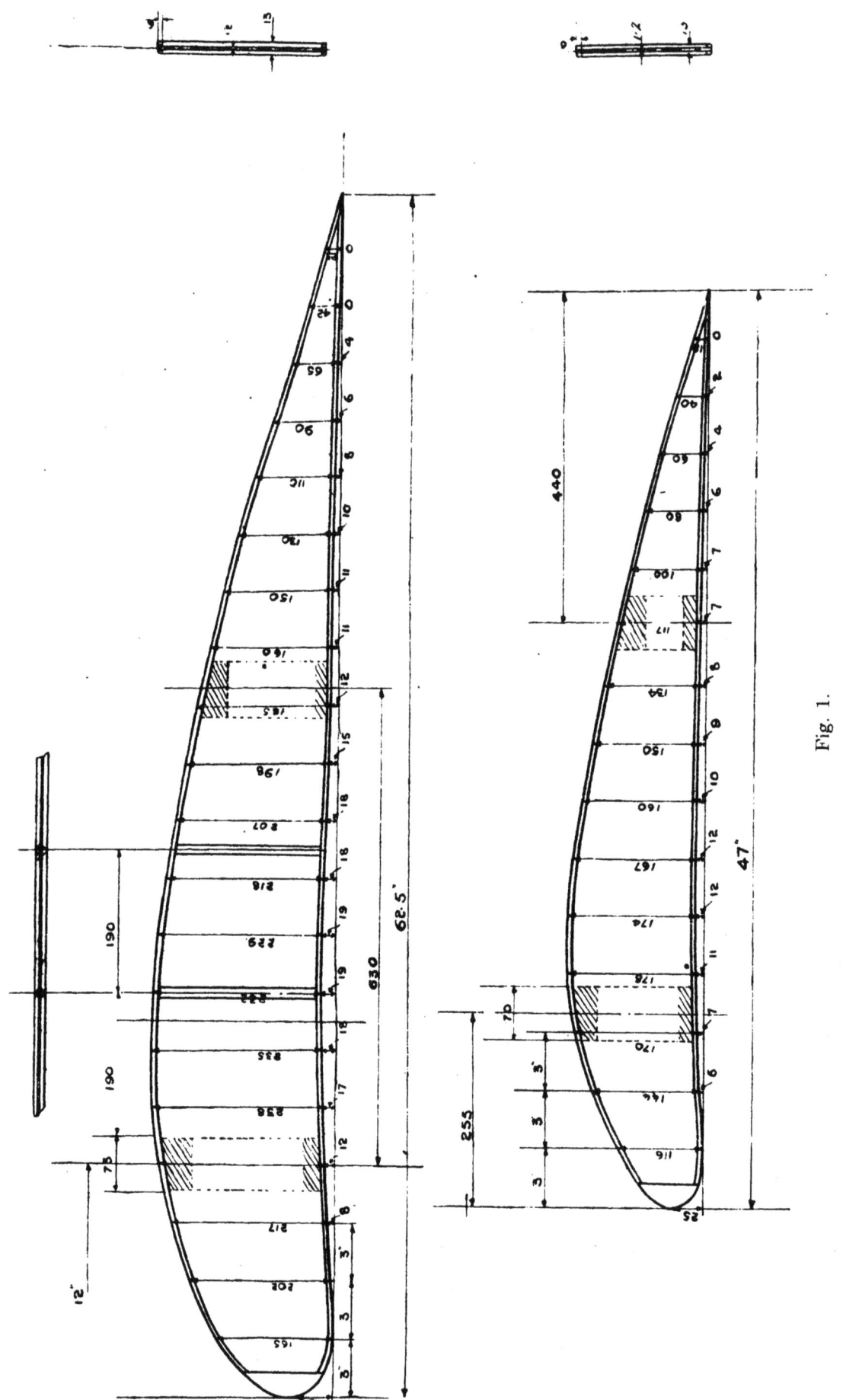

Fig. 1.

WING CONSTRUCTION.

In sharp contradistinction to the fuselage, which is constructed of steel, even including members where wood is almost universally used, the wings contain no metal parts, if we exclude strut fittings and other extraneous fixtures. There are no steel compression members, but where the internal wiring lugs occur, special box-form compression ribs are fixed. The leading edge is of very thin three-ply, which has a deeply serrated edge finishing on the main span (Fig. 1). The ribs are of three-ply, and are not lightened, although holes are, of course, cut where necessary, to accommodate the control and bracing wires. A rib from the top centre section, and one from the root of the lower wings, are both drawn to scale in Fig. 1.

The extreme thinness of the three-ply has given rise to a new method of fixing the flanges on the ribs. Instead of grooved flanges tacked on so that the tacks run down the length of the three-ply, two half flanges of approximately square section are tacked together horizontally with the ply sandwiched between (*see* Fig. 2).

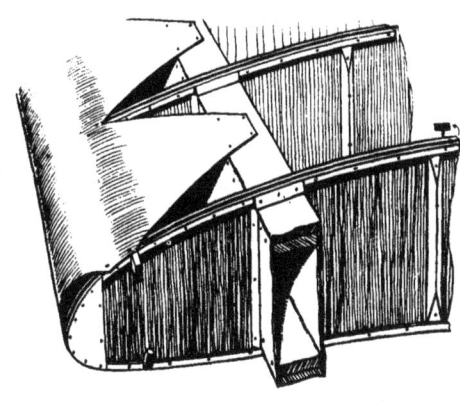

FIG. 2.

SPARS.

As may be seen from the various sections drawn to scale in Figs. 3 and 4, the spars are made up of fairly narrow flanges at top and bottom, joined on either side by thin three-ply webs. They are placed approximately 30 cms. apart. The flanges are made of Scots pine, and consist of two laminations. The three-ply has the two outer layers of birch and an inner ply which is probably birch also.

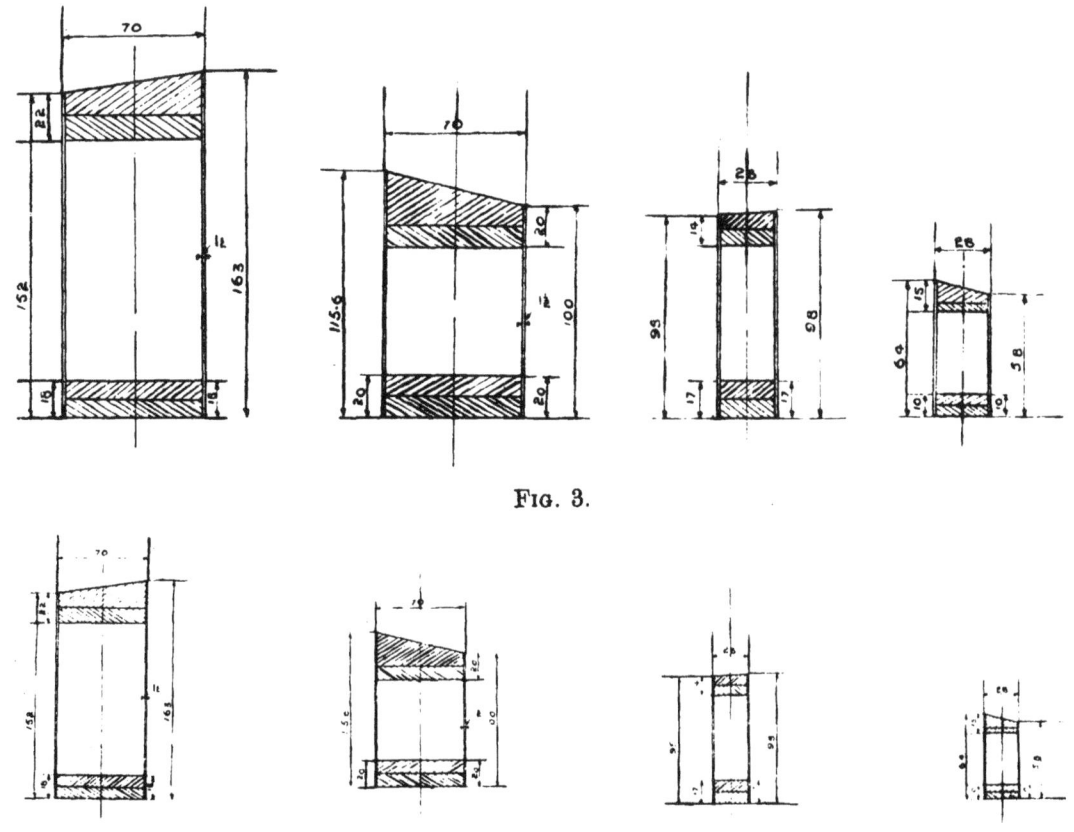

FIG. 3.

FIG. 4.

The three-ply webs are tacked on to the flanges, and fabric is glued over the joint. The cement is an ordinary gelatine glue.

The spar webs are glued to the flanges by a waterproof casein cement, which is proved to contain gelatine, while the ply wood adhesive—also a casein cement—is waterproof and of sufficiently good quality to withstand four hours' immersion in boiling water.

The trailing edge is of wire, and tape crosses from the top of one rib to the bottom of the next in the usual way. This tape lattice occurs about half-way between the trailing edge and the rear spar.

Fig. 3 shows the sections of the front and rear upper plane spars, taken in the centre section and at the interplane struts, while Fig. 4 gives the corresponding lower spar sections.

The ribs are stiffened between the spars by vertical pieces of wood of triangular section. There are two such pieces on each rib in the upper plane, and one in the lower plane.

All the woodwork of the wings is varnished, and fabric is bound round the flanges of the ribs and glued to the top and bottom of the spars.

The workmanship is decidedly good, and the finish neat and careful.

AILERONS.

As in the triplane, ailerons are fitted to the top wing only, and are of the same narrow shape. They are constructed of welded steel tubing. They conform to common German practice, in as much as they are fitted to a false spar well behind the rear spar, and are balanced. The welded up control lever follows British ideas, and does not work, as in most German designs, horizontally in a slot cut in the plane. All the tubing is lacquered.

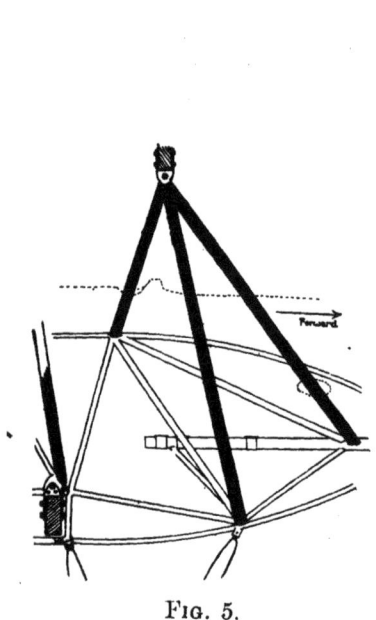

Fig. 5.

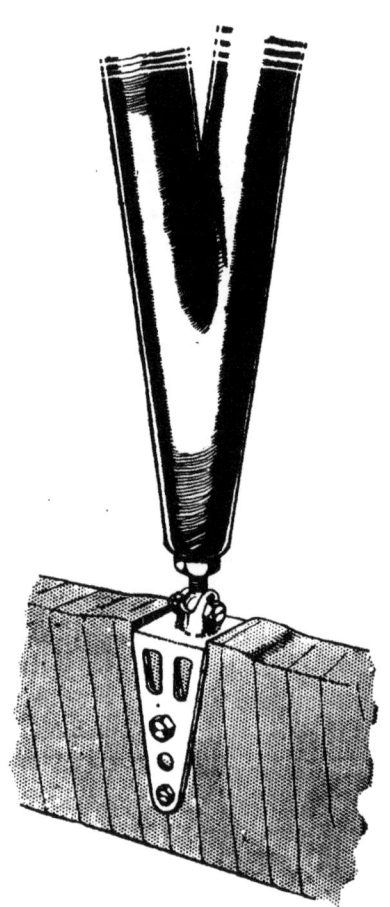

Fig. 6.

STRUTS.

The struts are all of steel tubing of streamline section, and the centre section system is particularly worthy of attention. All those three struts which meet at a point on the front spar of the upper wing are welded to the fuselage framework and are thus not removable when the machine is dismantled (see Fig. 5). The strut which joins the rear upper spar to the front lower spar, however, is not welded but is fastened by a ball and socket joint, which is the subject of Fig. 6.

It will be noticed that the ball forms the extremity of a threaded bolt which is screwed into the end of the strut, thus making it possible to adjust the length of the latter. Both ball and socket are drilled and a bolt locked through the hole. The attachment of upper centre section struts to the wing spar is shown in Fig. 7.

As is made clear in the scale drawings, the interplane struts are of N shape when seen from the starboard wing tip. The three members of the N are welded together, and all four free extremities have the adjustable attachment described above. It has already been mentioned that there is no external bracing, the wing construction being made sufficiently strong against lift stresses to obviate its necessity, and the form of the interplane struts is interesting in this connection.

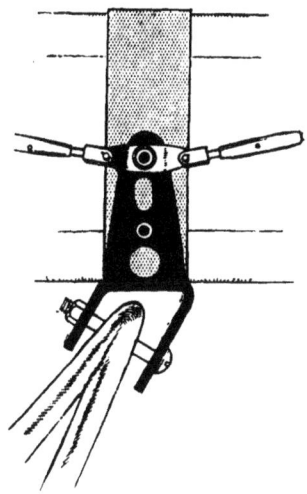

Fig. 7.

FUSELAGE.

This is exactly similar in design and construction to the triplane body—allowing, of course, for the difference in type of engine and for the fact that both wings have two spars instead of one. The longerons and cross struts are of circular section steel tube welded in place, and carrying at the corner the small quadrant of steel tube which carries the bracing. The diameters of these tubes vary from 22 mms. to 18 mms., and the steel was of 24 gauge in the places where the tubes had been pierced by bullets.

This bracing well repays attention. All sides of each section are cross-braced with piano wire, which is simply passed round the two lugs to be joined and has its extremities connected by means of a turnbuckle. This method has the great advantage that only two loops are required in the wire instead of four, and in consequence this bracing can be very rapidly assembled. It is also possibly lighter in relation to its strength than the usual arrangement of single wire bracing. Fig. 8 shows how a lifting handle is clipped on to the lower longerons.

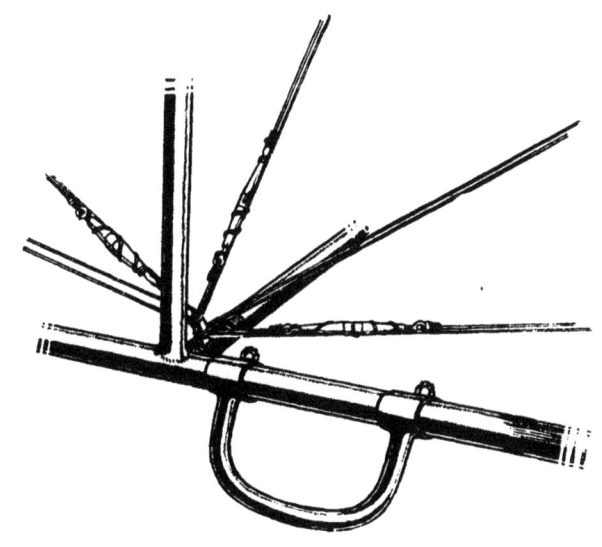

Fig. 8.

The front part of the body is a particularly good piece of welding, and includes the engine and radiator supports as well as the arrangement by which the continuous spars of the lower planes can be placed in position. This is done by removing two fork-ended tubes (one each side of the body), and replacing these when the wings are in position. Fig. 9 shows how the wing spar is joined to the fuselage, and Fig. 10 shows the fuselage joint at this point.

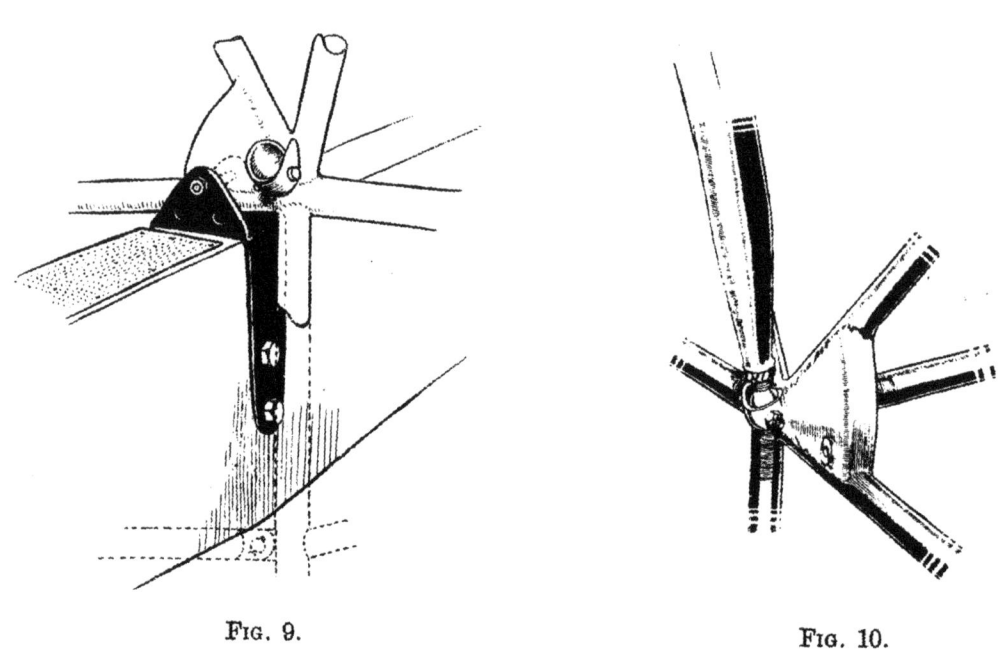

Fig. 9.   Fig. 10.

The cowling is of aluminium, and covers the front portion of the fuselage on all four sides. It is extended on the top to the cockpit, and underneath to beyond the rear spar. The cowls are arranged in convenient sheets, and are fastened by means of bolts and nuts of unusual shape. The nuts have small handles about 1" long, which enable one to manipulate them without tools. From the rear half of the cockpit to the junction of the tail and body, the top is furnished with a threeply fairing, which extends over not quite the whole width of the fuselage. This is shown in Fig. 11.

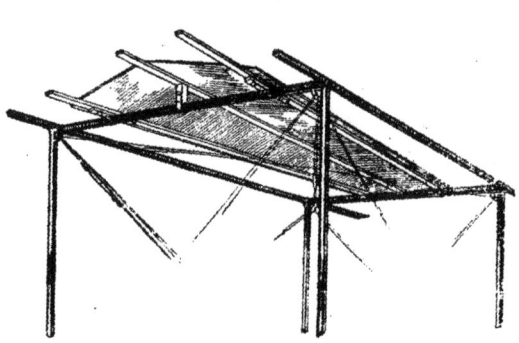

Fig. 11.

TAIL.

The fixed tail planes and elevators are almost similar to those of the triplane, i.e., the tail is triangular and the elevators balanced and divided, although they are actually made in one piece. The biplane, however, has a triangular fin whose foremost point is fixed an inch or two to the port side of the centre line of the machine, thus providing a surface which is inclined slightly to the longitudinal axis of the aeroplane. This is illustrated in Fig. 12, and is no doubt arranged to balance the tendency of the machine to turn to the left in flight, due to the slip-stream.

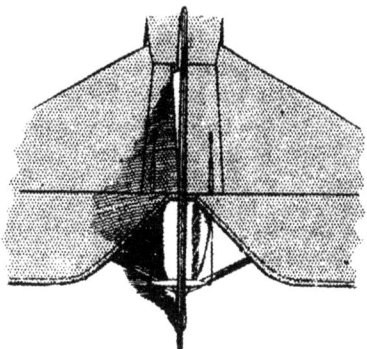

Fig. 12.

The framework of the tail is of circular section steel tubing throughout, including the trailing edges, and this framework is arranged to give the fixed tail plane a symmetrical camber. The attachment of the tail plane to the fuselage is simple and effective. As is the case in the triplane, the top longerons are dropped at this point sufficiently to allow the tail plane to have its top surface level with the top of the fuselage, and three bolts passing through the main steel tube of the tail and through short pieces of tube welded to the body framework secure it in this position. Of the three bolts, one is placed at either side of the top of the fuselage on the front of the tail, and one at the end of the body framework. The tail plane is set at a slight angle of incidence—about $3\frac{1}{2}°$—which is not intended to be adjustable, but which could easily be altered by means of a few washers and longer bolts. The tail is stayed by two streamline section steel struts, which connect the rear tube of the tail plane with the bottom of the sternpost, as is shown by the general arrangement drawings. These struts are not barbed.

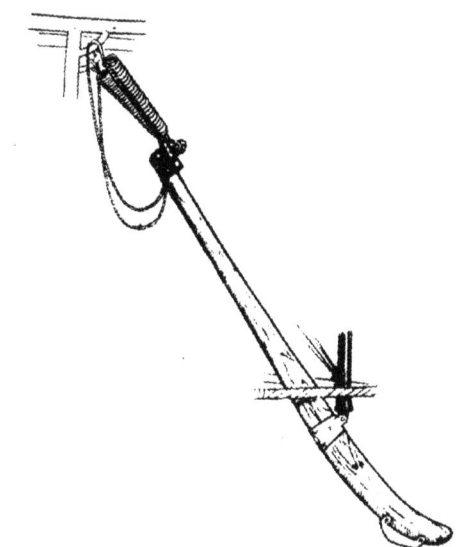

Fig. 13.

From the sketch of the tail skid (Fig. 13), it will be seen that this member is balanced at a point about one-third of its length from its lower end, and that the shock-absorbing arrangement consists of two helical steel springs.

UNDERCARRIAGE.

This is a feature of the machine which carries a distinct trace of British influence. The angle between the two limbs of the Vee is usually, in German aeroplanes, very obtuse; *i.e.*, the two top points of attachment are widely separated, while British practice leans towards making this angle fairly acute. In the Fokker the angle between the struts is about 55°. The section of the steel struts is streamline in form, with major and minor axes of 65 mms. and 34 mms. respectively. The metal is of 20 gauge.

The upper attachments of the undercarriage struts are of the ball and socket type, with a bolt through, similar to the interplane strut illustrated above. The junction of the lower extremities and the slot which allows for axle travel, is clearly explained by Fig. 14. The bracing cables, which connect the upper extremities of the front struts with the opposite lower ends, are attached in the usual manner to lugs welded on to the struts. It is interesting to note that in the crash which wrecked the machine, one of these lugs has torn out a small piece of the sheet steel of which the strut is formed, though there is no sign of fracture at the weld.

The least usual characteristic of the landing carriage, however, is the provision of a small cambered plane surrounding the axle, just as is the case in the Fokker triplane. This auxiliary plane has been badly battered, and few details are available, but the sheet aluminium box which surrounds the axle remains. This box is rectangular in section, and the edges are rivetted together on the upper side. It forms the main and only spar of the plane, the construction of which is very similar to that of the main plane. The shock absorbers are of the coil spring type, and are wrapped in the manner illustrated in Fig. 14. The wheels are 760 × 100.

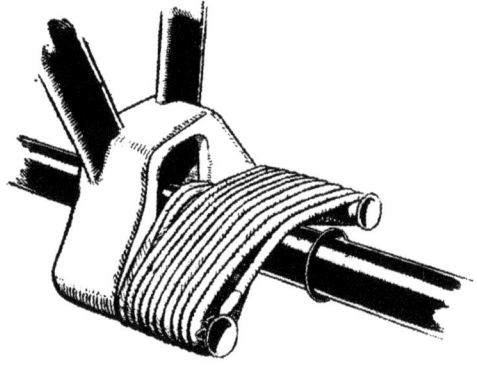

FIG. 14.

ENGINE AND MOUNTING.

The engine is a Mercedes of 180 H.P. A full report on this type of engine has already been issued, but the present example possesses one or two minor points of difference from the standard. The chief of these is the fact that this engine has domed pistons, giving higher compression. If found sufficiently interesting, the engine will shortly be reported upon separately.

As has already been mentioned, the engine bearers are steel tubes, supported on a steel tubular structure welded up integrally with the fuselage frame and with the centre section struts. The diameter of these two parallel tubes is 34 mms. and the gauge 14. Each tube carries four "pads" of the type shown in Fig. 15, to which the crankcase is bolted.

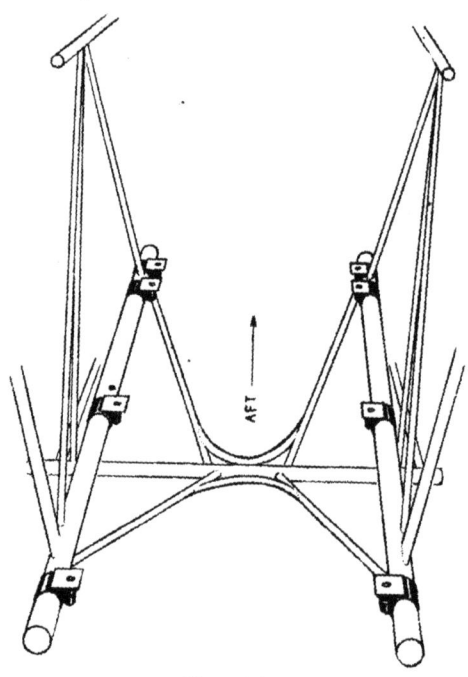

FIG. 15.

RADIATOR.

The radiator, as may be gathered from the scale drawings and sketches, is of the car type (another departure from modern German design), and is supported by steel tubes which are part of the fuselage frame. The radiating surface is surmounted by a curved fairing, of which the port-side half is a brass water tank, into which the filler leads, while the starboard side is merely an aluminium fairing. The radiator is constructed of brass tubes arranged parallel to the engine crankshaft. The tubes are circular in section, but expanded into hexagons at either end and sweated up there. Each hexagon measures 7 mms. across the flats.

The single shutter, as will be seen on reference to Fig. 16, is normally held open by a spring, but can be closed at will by pulling a small cable. This shutter even when completely closed only puts out of action a small portion (roughly about one-third) of the cooling surface.

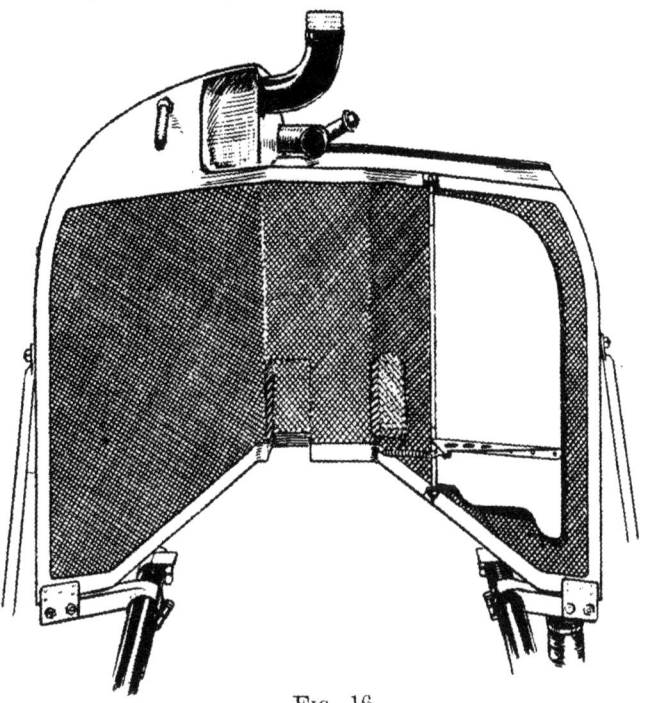

Fig. 16.

PETROL AND OIL SYSTEMS.

There is only one fuel and oil tank in the machine. It is of sheet brass and is slung from cross tubes clipped on to the top longerons, just in front of the ammunition magazines, which are placed immediately in front of the pilot.

So far as can be ascertained from such external evidence as is afforded by fillers, piping, the lines of rivets on the tank, and the gauges and petrol cocks, it may be said that this tank is divided into two petrol tanks and one oil tank. The main petrol tank has a capacity for 61 litres (approximately $13\frac{1}{2}$ galls.), and is provided with a baffle plate. The reserve tank holds 33 litres (approximately $7\frac{1}{4}$ galls.), while the oil tank carries $4\frac{1}{2}$ galls. From the brass disc which is sweated to each flank of the tank, it would appear that a tierod passes across the tank from side to side. Both petrol tanks work under pressure, obtained initially by hand pump and maintained by the usual mechanical air pump. The dashboard carries, besides the main switches and a starting magneto, a two-way cock which allows the pilot to use petrol from the main or auxiliary tank, or to shut it off completely. A separate pressure gauge for each tank and two two-way air pressure cocks are also mounted. Fig. 17 is a diagram of the dashboard with the original German descriptions translated. The " Achtung, Hohengas " appears to be simply a warning to the pilot not to forget the extra air control. It does not seem to bear any relation to any instrument on the dash.

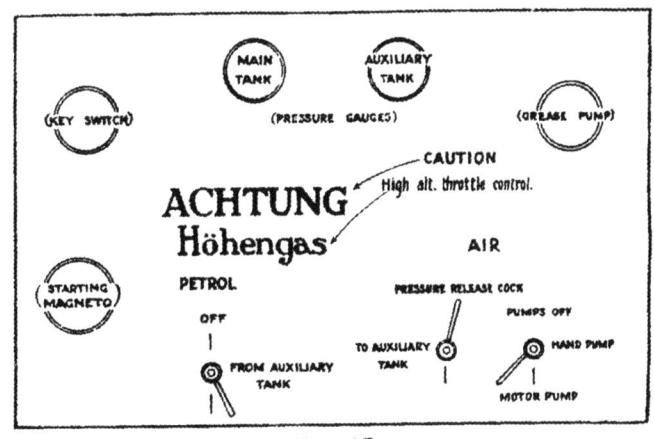

Fig. 17.

THROTTLE CONTROL.

A sketch of the throttle lever, situated on the pilot's left, is given (Fig. 18). This lever actuates the carburetter throttle by the means shown. The compression tube between the quadrant and the balanced lever is over 4 ft. long and about ⅜ in. in diameter. Although heavy-looking, this control is, of course, made of very light gauge material. The adjustment provided at the pilot's end of the control should be noticed. This control works in conjunction with a Bowden type lever on the control lever, as shown by Fig. 18. The twin cables from this auxiliary throttle lever are attached to the main throttle control—Fig. 18 shows the attachments.

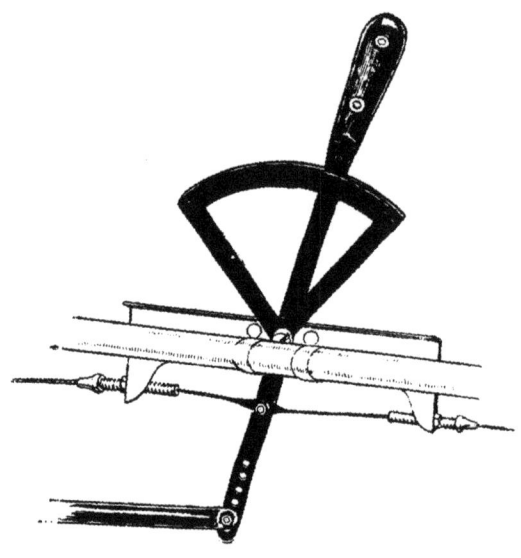

Fig. 18.

CONTROLS.

The control lever of the machine works on precisely the same system as that of the triplane, but the grip at the head of the column is quite different. Reference to Fig. 19 will show that the usual two-handed grip is replaced by a single handle for the right hand.

The left hand is free to manipulate the auxiliary throttle control, inter-connected with the main throttle lever. It should also be noticed that the usual pushes for firing the guns are absent, and the interrupter gear is actuated by pulling either or both of the levers by the fingers, while the thumb rests on the specially arranged place. There is no separate arrangement for firing both guns together, and it is not possible to lock the elevator controls in any given position.

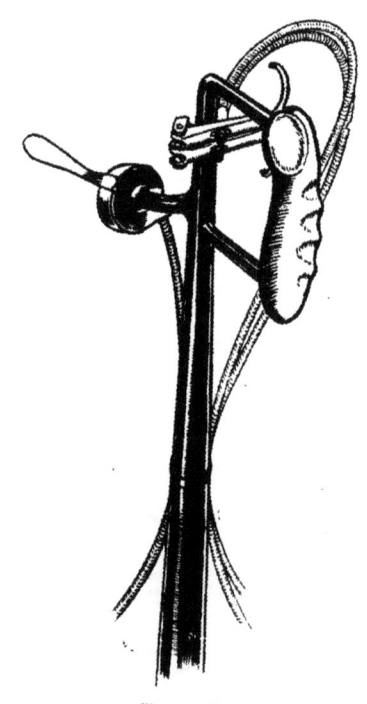

Fig 19.

The longitudinal rocking shaft carries at its front end two arms to which the aileron control cables are fixed (*see* Fig. 20). These wires cross; and pass upwards and outwards to aluminium pulleys on ball bearings, which are attached in pairs to a hinged sheet steel framework. On the way these cables pass through short tubular guides fixed to the top longerons. The aileron levers follow contemporary British practice, and project vertically above and below the plane.

The elevator control wires are taken direct from the control lever, one pair above and one pair below the fulcrum.

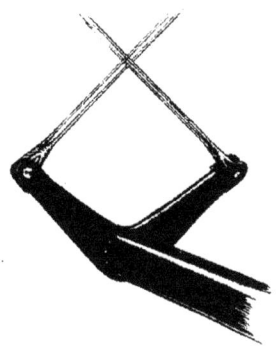

Fig. 20.

The rudder bar (*see* Fig. 21) is of neat and light welded construction. There is no adjustment to allow for variation in leg-length of different pilots, but it should be noticed that the pilot's seat is adjustable as regards height. The means by which this movement is obtained is exactly the same as the arrangement in the triplane, *i.e.*, the seat is a sheet aluminium bucket with a three-ply bottom supported by a framework of steel tubes which grips the fuselage cross struts by four clips, which can be placed at any height. This is made clear by Fig. 22.

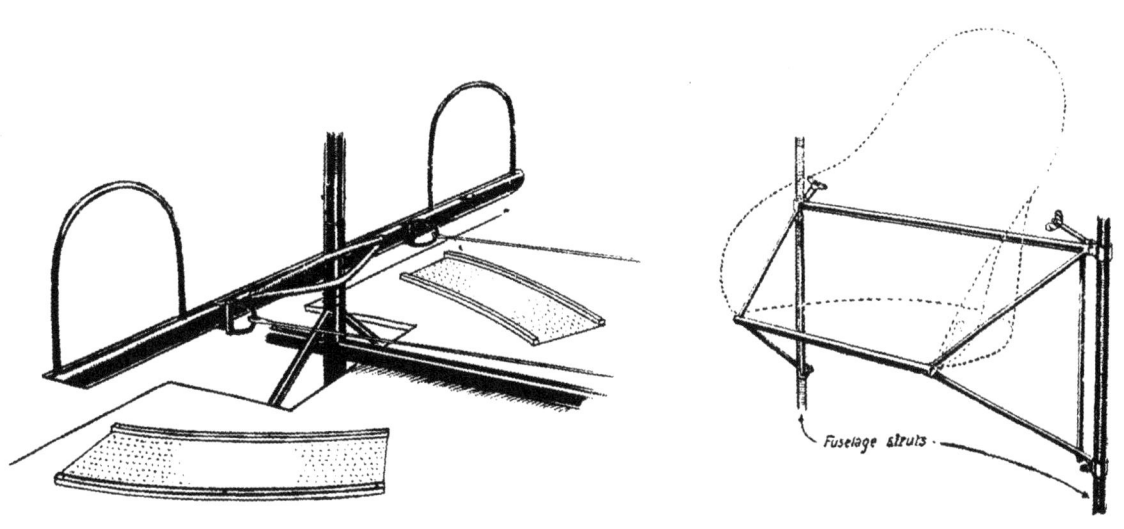

Fig. 21.   Fig. 22.

ARMAMENT.

This presents no unusual feature. Two fixed Spandau guns (Nos. 5,085 and 4,829) fire through the propeller path in the usual way. The working of the triggers operating the clutches of the interrupter gear has already been described.

The ammunition magazines and chutes are made of sheet aluminium, and the whole of the gun mechanism is within easy reach of the pilot.

FABRIC AND DOPE.

The fabric is not attached in any way to the longerons, but is simply carried over the fuselage and laced along the bottom central line. There is a cross-piece of fabric laced to the cross tubes immediately behind the cockpit.

The fabric is coarse flax, coarser and less highly calendered than the type usually met with, and a good deal heavier.

It is colour-printed in the usual irregular polygons. The bright red paint, mentioned below, is removable by alcohol, but not soluble in it, coming off as a skin under the treatment.

Under the paint is a dope layer—an acetyl cellulose. Neither paint nor dope presents unusual features.

Weights—
Paint	...	92.0 gms. per sq. m.
Dope	...	68.1 ,, ,, ,, ,,
Fabric	...	143.6 ,, ,, ,, ,,
		303.7 ,, ,, ,, ,,
Strength	...	1772 k/m.
Extension	...	7.0%

Where the wings are not painted, the fabric is covered with a thin layer of dope only.

The colouring of the machine is interesting. The top surface of the wings is painted a brilliant vermillion, while on the underneath surfaces the fabric is untouched, and is revealed as the familiar printed-colour fabric. The body is red in the front portion—where are the aluminium cowls—except the radiator, which is painted white. From the cockpit to the rear the colour is white.

The vertical surfaces of the tail are also white, and the horizontal surfaces—on both top and bottom—black

SCHEDULE OF PRINCIPAL WEIGHTS.

	lbs.	oz
Upper wing, complete with ailerons, pulleys, bracing wires, fabric and strut fittings	156	0
Lower wing (no ailerons fitted), complete with strut fittings and fabric	97	0
N strut between wings	6	9
Straight strut, between fuselage and trailing spar of upper wing	2	8
Aileron frame, with hinge clips, without fabric	4	8
Rudder frame, with hinge clips, without fabric	4	11
Fin frame, without fabric	1	14
Tail planes (complete in one piece), without fabric	12	6
Elevators (complete in one piece), without fabric	11	2
Radiator, empty	48	0
Undercarriage strut, each	2	10
Undercarriage axle, with shock absorber bobbins	18	2
Bobbin, each	0	7
Shock absorber, each	3	9
Undercarriage (complete), without wheels and tyres, and without plane, but including struts	29	4
Aluminium tube, forming rear spar of undercarriage plane	1	8
Wheel, without tyre and tube	11	8
Tyre and tube	9	4
Tail strut	1	15
Fabric, per square foot, with dope	0	1
Bottom plane compression rib	0	15
Bottom plane ordinary rib	0	11
Top plane ordinary rib, at centre of plane	1	0
Bracket, with bolts, attaching top plane to fuselage struts	1	11
Main spar, top plane, including fillets for ribs, per foot run in centre	1	12

Owing to tapering ends the average weight per foot of the spars will be slightly less than this figure.

This aeroplane is at the Enemy Aircraft View Rooms, Islington, and may be seen on production of a pass to be obtained by a written application to :—The Controller, Technical Dept. Ap.D.(L.), Central House, Kingsway, W.C.2.

W.G.A.

J. G. WEIR,

Brig.-General,

Controller, Technical Department.

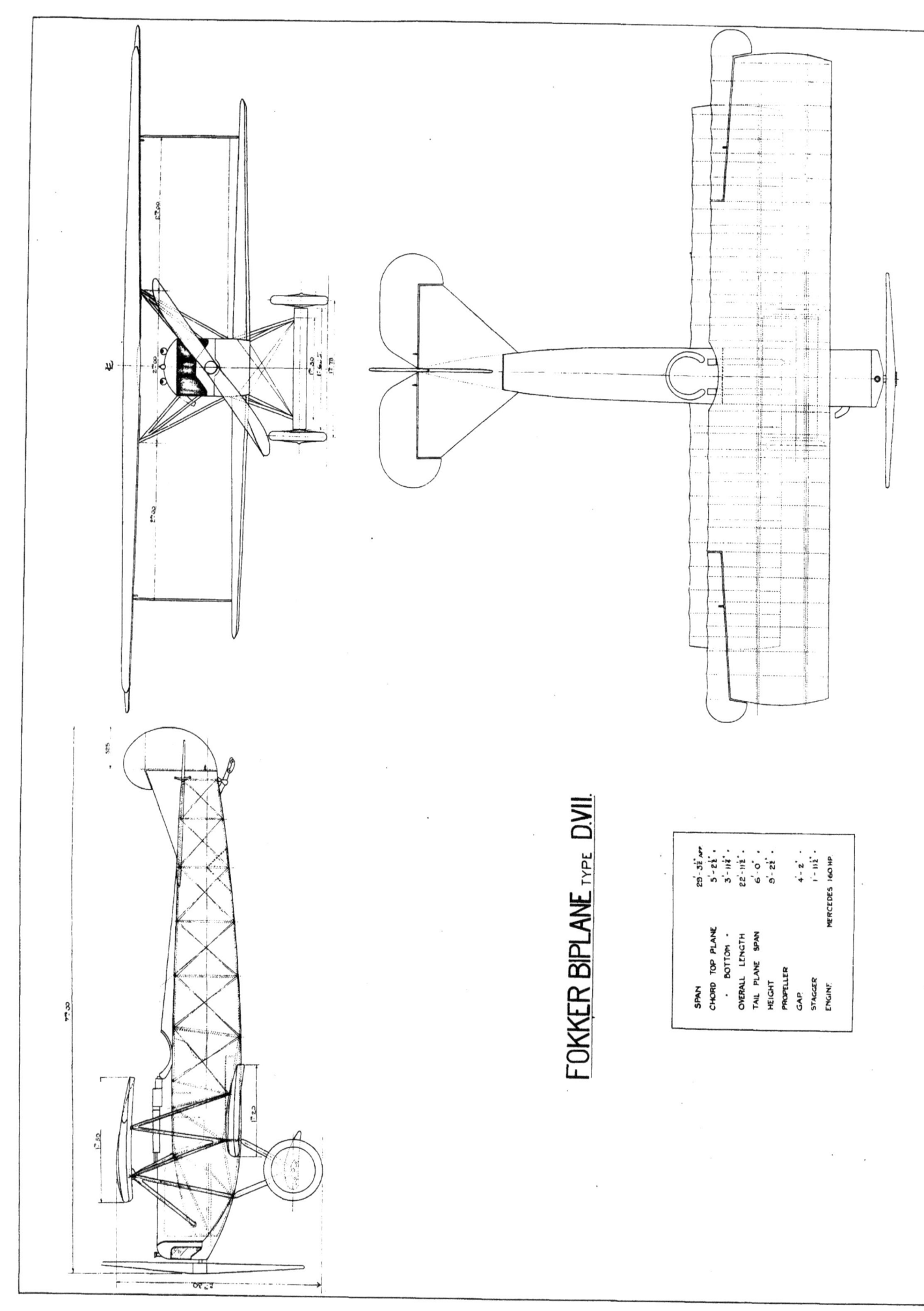

www.ingramcontent.com/pod-product-compliance
Ingram Content Group UK Ltd.
Pitfield, Milton Keynes, MK11 3LW, UK
UKHW051525180426
11947UKWH00019B/1589